The Importance of Possibili…

R
8-4-'08

P. A. Sheehan   6.4.'08

ABOUT THE AUTHOR

Edward de Bono has been called 'the father of thinking about thinking'. He is the originator of the concept – and formal tools – of Lateral Thinking. He is regarded by many as the leading authority in the field of creative thinking, innovation and the direct teaching of thinking as a skill.

His methods are taught in thousands of schools around the world and his instruction in thinking has been sought by many business organisations over the years, including IBM, Prudential, Shell, Nokia, Bank of America and GM. He is on the Accenture list of the fifty most influential business thinkers in the world.

Dr de Bono was born in Malta. He was a Rhodes Scholar at Oxford, holds an M.A. in psychology and physiology from Oxford, a D. Phil. in Medicine, a Ph.D. from Cambridge, a D. Des. (Doctor of Design) from the Royal Melbourne Institute of Technology and an LL.D. from Dundee. He holds professorships at the Universities of Malta and Pretoria, Dublin City University and the University of Central England.

The Importance of Possibili…

Edward de Bono
(inventor of lateral thinking)

BP

BLACKHALL
PUBLISHING

This book was typeset by Ark Imaging for

BLACKHALL PUBLISHING
33 Carysfort Avenue
Blackrock
Co. Dublin
Ireland
e-mail: info@blackhallpublishing.com
www.blackhallpublishing.com

© 2007 The McQuaig Group, Inc.
ISBN 978-1-84218-134-8

Printed in the United Kingdom by Cromwell Press

There is a possibility that the word on the cover of the book should be:

POSSIBILITY

There is a high probability that this is the word.

There can even be certainty if you know the language to be English and there is no other word that could fit.

Why do we pay so little attention to the importance of 'possibility'?

There might be many reasons but I shall only deal with some of them here.

The first reason is that no one in the whole course of our education has told us that 'possibility' is very important.

The second reason is that we regard possibility as very inferior to 'truth' or 'fact'.

This is all very understandable. You have to act on truth or fact. When you go to the supermarket you have to buy some definite food items. You can think of possibilities but you pay cash for the certainty of the food in your basket at the check-out point.

If you are a wild animal you need to be certain that the other animal approaching you is a predator – then you run away.

If you are having a house built you need to know the definite cost. It is very hard to plan for 'possible' costs.

Action needs certainty.

Interaction needs certainty.

Belief needs certainty.

If you are going to die for a cause you need to know for sure that it is a good cause — possibility is not enough.

STEPS AND END

At the end of our thinking we want 'certainty' and 'truth' because that is what we are going to act upon.

If the end has to be certain it makes sense for every step towards the end also to be certain. With a logical progression of steps, each of which is certain, we arrive at an end point which must also be certain.

This is a very natural ambition. The huge influence of the GG3 (Greek Gang of Three – Socrates, Plato and Aristotle) on our thinking confirmed and reinforced this natural desire for certainty.

If you are driving north it makes sense that at any moment you are moving in that direction. Does it really make sense?

Consider the simple road arrangement shown in the diagram . . . You are intending to travel from A to B. The point B is north of A. To get to B you have to go south to begin with. Seeking to move north at every moment would prevent you ever getting to B.

The end result of our thinking may indeed need to be certain but the steps for getting there can be different. In many cases they have to be different because they have to include 'possibility'.

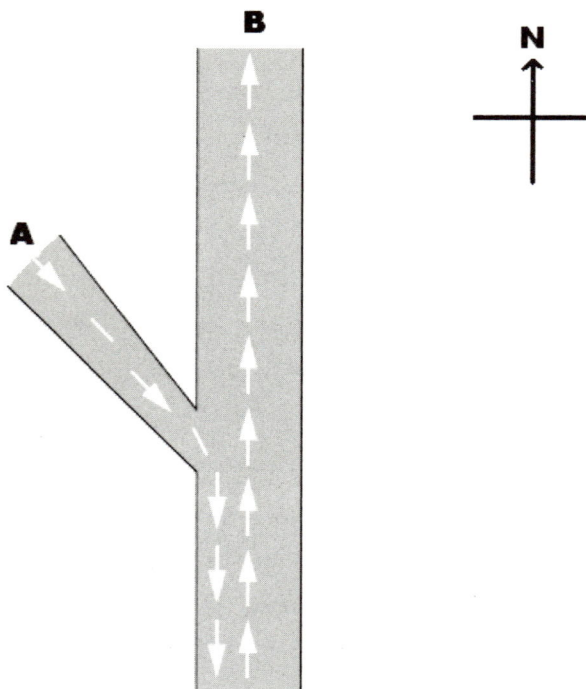

WHAT HAPPENED TO CHINA?

Two thousand years ago, China was far ahead of the West in science and technology. They had rockets and gunpowder and various other things.

Had China continued to progress at the same rate, today China would easily be the dominant power in the world – scientifically, technically, economically and militarily.

So what happened?

There are various theories and here are two of them.

The first is that Chinese imperial culture reached such a state of 'perfection' that they believed that any change would be for the worse. Self-organising systems do reach states of 'local equilibrium'. Any change out of that state is difficult and (for the moment) negative and disruptive.

A second explanation is that the scholars, who were very dominant in Chinese culture, started to believe that you could move from 'certainty' to 'certainty' and there was no need for the messiness of possibility.

As a result they never developed the possibility system (which includes hypothesis) and progress came to a dead end.

THE INFORMATION AGE

Exactly what happened to China is happening in the rest of the world today. The result may well be the same. That is, stagnation.

Because of the excellence of our computers and telecommunication systems we can collect and transmit information.

We then proceed to analyse this information for meaning, trends, patterns, etc.

As a result we see no need for possibility or creative thinking. The logic of the information determines our decisions, our strategies and all our thinking.

This is indeed what is happening.

Recently I was told by the creative head of one of the world's major advertising agencies that clients no longer wanted ideas. They just wanted the research data and they would react to this.

Is there anything wrong with this adoration of data and reliance upon it?

No. It is needed and an excellent trend.

But it is not sufficient. The rear left wheel of a motorcar is excellent.

There is nothing wrong with it at all. By itself, however, the rear wheel is not enough.

So data by itself is not enough.

We need creative possibilities to be able to look at the data in different ways.

We need creative possibilities to put this data together with other data to design value.

We need creative possibilities to imagine where or how we could look for more data.

Data without possibilities is like food without a cook.

It is never a matter of reducing the need for or attention to data. It is a matter of realising that data does not exclude the need for 'possibility'.

THE POWER OF POSSIBILITY

Peptic ulcers include both stomach ulcers and duodenal ulcers. It is a major condition affecting thousands of people.

People with this condition used to have a miserable life.

They had to watch carefully every mouthful they ate. They had to keep off spicy foods. They had to reduce the intake of alcohol. Some of them were on rigidly controlled diets.

They had to keep taking antacid medicines all the time, sometimes for twenty years or more. The medicine was necessary to control the burning and gnawing pain in their stomach.

There were major operations such as Billroth's operations. These operations removed part or all of your stomach in order to cure the condition by removing the 'cause'.

A high number of hospital beds were occupied by patients under treatment or diagnosis for the condition.

There were complications such as severe gastro-intestinal bleeding and perforated ulcers.

So it was a major condition. And a lot of people were doing a lot of thinking about it.

Then in Perth, Western Australia, a young doctor named Barry J. Marshall thought of a 'possibility'.

He suggested that a peptic ulcer was the result of an 'infection'. He suggested that the infecting agent was the Helicobacter pylori.

Everyone laughed – out loud or in their minds.

How could it be an infection when the very strong hydrochloric acid in the stomach would surely kill any bacteria?

Dr Marshall made a culture of the bacteria he suspected and drank it. He gave himself a peptic ulcer. No one was convinced.

Many, many, many years later it turns out that he was right.

Instead of twenty years on antacids.

Instead of losing all or some of your stomach.

Instead of occupying all those hospital beds.

Instead of leading a rather miserable life.

You just take antibiotics for one week and you are cured!

That is the power of possibility.

THE HYPOTHESIS

All scientists acknowledge the huge importance of the hypothesis. This was also an invention of the ancient Greek thinkers – but before the GG3.

The hypothesis sets up a frame of 'possibility' which then directs our search for more information. The frame allows us to design experiments.

According to Karl Popper, a rather famous philosopher, we should seek the most reasonable hypothesis and then try to prove it wrong (not try to prove it right). This makes sense up to a point.

But if you only have the most reasonable hypothesis you can only look at the evidence from one point of view.

You need the possibility of several hypotheses at the same time – even some that seem bizarre. That is why Barry J. Marshall solved the problem of a major condition that had not yielded to 'reasonable' hypotheses.

Although all scientists acknowledge the importance of hypotheses, very little is done about it. The scientific method is all about data and the analysis of data.

The hypothesis is like an uncouth cousin who has to be invited to family parties but no one pays much attention to.

When I was younger I spent time at the universities of Oxford, Cambridge, London and Harvard. These are major universities with a well-earned reputation for excellence.

I have to say that, in my experience at least, no time at all was spent on the importance of possibility and the hypothesis.

Why?

The answer is surprisingly simple.

How much data do you need to set up a reasonable hypothesis? You are not allowed just to pluck a hypothesis from the air.

What is not realised is that the collection of the preliminary data, and the way that it is looked at, depends on existing hypotheses. This makes it difficult to generate really new hypotheses. At the same time people do not want to be wasting time on 'mad' hypotheses.

Recently, Australia had the lowest rate of marriage there had been for one hundred years. What is your hypothesis?

Recently Spain had the lowest birth rate in Europe. This is surprising because Spain is a Catholic country and contraceptive measures are frowned upon. What is your hypothesis?

China is the only country where the suicide rate for women exceeds the rate for men. What is your hypothesis?

WHAT IS AND WHAT CAN BE

The hypothesis is a tool in our search for the truth.

You can have truth about the past and about the present. Science seeks to discover eternal truths that were valid yesterday, today and forever into the future.

There is a fat man and a thin man and they are running against each other. It is not a race. Perhaps they are running after the girls.

The thin man always wins.

What can the fat man do?

There are three approaches.

The first approach is the classification approach. We use this method in psychiatry, psychology, medicine, botany, etc. We label standard situations. Then we seek to identify the standard 'box' into which something ought to be placed.

Once something is in the box then we know all about it and how to deal with it – as in a medical diagnosis. If we diagnose you as having measles we know the probable course of the illness and what to do about it.

So we put the fat man into 'fat man box'. We tell him that fat men do not run fast. That is his nature. That is his behaviour. That is his destiny. It may even be his genes. Too bad.

The second approach is the analysis approach. We analyse why the fat man cannot run faster. We conclude that it is because of his weight and even his configuration.

The next step in the analysis is to decide what we are going to do about it. We put the fat man on a diet and tell him that if he sticks to the diet, sometime in the future he might be able to run faster than the thin man.

The third approach is the one we use very rarely. It is the 'design' approach.

We put the fat man on a bicycle and he will certainly outperform the thin man.

The design approach is not about 'what is' but all about 'what can be'.

Throughout education we teach analysis. We never teach design. Yet design is as key a part of progress as analysis and truth.

Design is all about 'possibility'.

In design you think about a possible value. You think about a possible function. You think about a possible outcome. Then you think about possible ways of getting the value, the function or the outcome.

You test these possible ways against information, knowledge and reality. But you have to think of them as possibilities first of all!

Design is a sort of 'forward hypothesis'. It is not about 'what might be' but about 'what can be' in the future.

PERCEPTION

This is a very important area.

Ever since the GG3 we have been taught that thinking is all about recognising a standard situation and providing the standard response. One hundred per cent of education is about this.

We have also been taught that thinking is all about information and logical deduction.

All this is equivalent to making a gin and tonic without the gin.

The key part of thinking in everyday life is 'perception'.

David Perkins at Harvard did research which supports this point of view. He showed that ninety per cent of the errors in thinking were errors of perception. Errors of logic accounted for a small ten per cent.

How we see the world in perception determines our judgements and our actions.

It is even worse than that. Gödel's theorem shows that from within a system you can never logically prove the starting points. So no matter how much you pride yourself on the excellence of your logic, in the end it will all depend on arbitrary perceptions and values.

In Australia a five-year-old was offered by his friends a choice between a one-dollar coin and a two-dollar coin. In Australia the one-dollar coin is much bigger than the two-dollar coin.

The boy took the one-dollar coin. His friends laughed and giggled. Wasn't Johnny stupid to take the lower-value coin just because it was larger?

So whenever they wanted to make a fool of Johnny they offered him the two coins. He always took the larger one. He never seemed to learn.

One day an adult saw this and called Johnny over.

'Believe me,' he told Johnny, 'the smaller coin is worth twice as much as the bigger coin – even though it is smaller.'

Johnny listened very politely. Then he replied:

'Yes. I know that. But how often would they have offered me the two coins if I had taken the two-dollar coin the first time?'

It was a matter of perception. If Johnny had seen it as a 'once only' situation he might well have taken the smaller coin.

Because he knew his friends and how they would like to go on teasing him, he saw it as a 'repeat' situation. In the process he made much more money.

Many of the programmes I have designed for use in school and elsewhere are to do with improving perception. These include CoRT (Cognitive Research Trust) and DATT (Direct Attention Thinking Tools).

A class of thirty twelve-year-old boys were asked if it would be a good idea for them to be paid to go to school. All thirty of them decided it would be a good idea.

Then a very simple perceptual scanning tool was explained to them. After using this tool the result was completely different. Twenty-nine out of the thirty decided it would not be a good idea at all.

Two hundred and fifty top women executives were asked if it would be a good idea for women to be paid fifteen per cent more than men for doing the same job. Eighty-six per cent were in favour and claimed they needed more money because they had more responsibilities. Another, very simple, perceptual scanning tool was introduced. The number in favour dropped from eighty-six per cent to just fifteen per cent.

In a South African platinum mine there used to be two hundred and ten fights every month between the seven tribes working there. After the illiterate miners had been taught some very simple perceptual scanning tools the number of fights dropped from two hundred and ten to just four.

In London youngsters who are too violent to be taught in normal schools get sent to the Hungerford Guidance Centre. Many years ago the principal, David Lane, started teaching perceptual thinking tools to the youngsters. In a twenty-year follow-up he has now shown that those youngsters taught thinking had an actual criminal conviction rate of one tenth that of those not taught thinking.

Perception is very, very powerful and very, very important – and almost completely neglected by traditional education.

Perception is very much about possibility.

We look at a situation and quickly decide what it is and how to interpret it. There is a rush to certainty and 'truth'.

Yet if there is a pause to consider other possibilities and alternative ways of looking at the situation, then the results can be very different, as illustrated in the dramatic results given above.

What are the possibilities here? How else could I look at the situation?

What are the results of opening up these new possible perceptions? There could be several results.

Firstly, we might suddenly see the situation in a different way. Once seen in this way it becomes obvious that it could be so. A difficult child could be seen to be insecure rather than aggressive for example. A crying woman may be seen to be exploitative rather than pitiful for example.

Secondly, we seek to check out the possibilities in some way. This is similar to the role of the hypothesis in science. We might need to ask questions or to get more information to see which of the possibilities is the most probable.

Thirdly, if we cannot decide which possibility is the most likely, then we have to design our response to cover the different possibilities. So the response would be appropriate for any of the possibilities.

What we must not do is to throw out possibilities because we want certainty. That way you may appear to get certainty but it may well be a false and dangerous certainty.

The rush to certainty in perception is very limiting and very dangerous.

The habit of opening up perceptual possibilities is not difficult and can be developed. The specific perceptual tools, now taught in many schools, are a great help in this respect (e.g. the CoRT programme).

AN EYE FOR POSSIBILITIES

I was once teaching thinking to a class made up entirely of Nobel Prize winners.

Only one of those present had arrived at his or her breakthrough idea by systematic analysis. Every other person had reached the idea as a result of chance, mistake, anomaly or something going wrong.

All these things would have been ignored by most people. But each of those people had 'an eye for possibilities'. Because something was not what was expected there was a need to explore the possibilities. There were the possibilities of how it came about. There were the possibilities of what it indicated about the underlying system. There were the possibilities of what new ideas it could lead to.

In traditional thinking you need to be right at each step so that your end result is necessarily right.

In 'provocation' there may not be a reason for saying something until after it has been said.

Provocation is part of the formal process of lateral thinking. Lateral thinking is based on an understanding of the brain as a self-organising information system. Such systems make patterns. Pattern-making systems are always asymmetric.

From this arises the formal tools of lateral thinking.

Provocation is one of them. The word 'Po' is a word I invented to signal a provocation.

With lateral thinking the statement does not have to be true. It does not even have to be a possibility.

We might say, 'Po, cars have square wheels.' This would seem complete nonsense to an engineer.

Yet from this provocation comes the idea of 'anticipatory suspension' where the suspension acts in advance of actual need. Such vehicles ride smoothly over rough ground while the wheel follows the profile of the ground.

Mathematicians agree that in any self-organising system provocation is needed – otherwise you get stuck in a local equilibrium.

Once the provocation is there then you use the mental process called 'movement' to move forward to new possibilities and new ideas.

I was once taken out to the desert in Arizona. There are many large cacti there. The surface of the cactus is covered with small spines.

The usual explanation is that the spines prevent animals from eating the plant.

Yet there are animals in many other parts of the world and plants in these parts do not develop spines — though they should for protection.

Maybe the spines serve another purpose.

Maybe the spines keep the boundary layer of air, next to the surface of the plant, quite still. The result is that there is much less evaporation of water and the plant needs less water. Which is rather important in a desert.

A fan cools a person down by providing a moving current of air, which causes evaporation of sweat and so cools us down. The effect of the spines is exactly the opposite. To stop the movement of air and so stop loss of water.

Many entrepreneurs get going because they have an eye for possibilities.

They notice a new need which no one else has noticed and then set up satisfying that need – at a profit.

Or, the entrepreneur notices the way something is done and thinks of another 'possible' way of doing it. So the outcome may be the same but the process and costs are much less – with more profit as a result.

We are trained to seek truth and certainty. We should also be trained to look for possibilities. The two are no more contradictory than having fish at one meal and meat at the next meal.

FORECASTING

By definition, forecasting is all about the future. That means there is uncertainty. That means there are possibilities.

Present day trends may give us some sense of certainty about the future. There is a trend towards global warming. That is likely to continue. There is a movement of rural populations into towns. There is a growing shortage of fresh water. There is an ever-increasing demand for energy.

Politicians have to make forecasts all the time.

'If I say this, how will people react – and the media?'

With any new law or regulation there is a need to forecast how it will be received and how people will react to it.

Many years ago China introduced a 'one child policy'. This meant that families were only allowed to have one child.

For various practical and cultural reasons, families felt they needed a boy child. So, somehow, the girl children disappeared. Today it is estimated that there is a shortage of one hundred million women in China.

Now it may be that this was precisely foreseen as a possibility, given Chinese culture. This means that the population will decline ever more sharply because of the shortage of women.

Perhaps it was not foreseen as a possibility.

A different idea would have been to let families have as many children as they wanted – until they had a boy. Then they should stop having further children.

The result of this approach would be equal boys and girls (because at conception there is an equal chance of conceiving either sex). There would also be, on average, two children per family, which is less than replacement, which needs about 2.3 children per family. This might have been a better approach.

Some countries, like Slovakia, are introducing a flat rate of income tax. Other countries are very interested in seeing the 'possibilities' of how this might work out.

As 'truth' is to the past so 'possible values' are to the future.

If you can think of a possibility you can examine its likelihood and its effects. If you cannot think of a possibility then you are driving in the dark.

POSSIBILITY RATINGS

There is some value in having possibility 'ratings' – so long as you do not use them.

Some possibilities are clearly more 'probable' than others. The danger is that if we start rating them then the temptation is to throw out and ignore the less probable. That is dangerous.

There is the stage of action or decision when we do need to focus on the 'more probable' possibilities. But it is only at this final stage of thinking.

The temptation is to apply the ratings right at the beginning and so throw out the least probable possibilities, which may, sometimes, be the most valuable.

Any rating of possibilities is necessarily based on our current knowledge, current thinking and current hypotheses. Yet it is the least likely possibilities that may serve to change our thinking. They cannot do this if they are thrown out at the beginning of our thinking.

So the danger is that we simply reinforce our existing thinking by using it to select possibilities that agree with that thinking.

It seems to be a dilemma: we should not throw out remote possibilities and yet we have to act on the most probable. In fact, it is not a dilemma at all. Our thinking should encompass all possibilities, even the remote ones, but when we come to action we now need to focus on the more probable.

It often happens that in the course of our thinking a remote possibility becomes a distinct probability. If that remote possibility had been thrown out at the beginning this could never have happened.

I once wrote a book titled *Why I Want to be King of Australia*. The book was well received. In it I argue the logical case of why Australia needs a king of its own (not a boring president of a republic) and why I would be a good choice to get the system going. Then I would abdicate.

What sort of possibility is this? Even though most Australians have a great sense of humour and initiative, I do not believe the possibility to be very high.

In a rating system we would place this possibility at the bottom – as a remote possibility.

But what about more remote possibilities? The possibility that pigs can fly. The possibility that gravity might one day be reversed and everything would fly off the surface of the earth. The possibility that all human skin would turn purple. The possibility that a mouse could give birth to an elephant. The possibility that men could become superfluous and unnecessary.

Because we can put together words to express something does not make it a possibility. It is just possible that we could in the future somehow combine the DNA of a mouse and an elephant – but a mouse (as we know it) could not give birth to an elephant (as we know it).

The possibility that men could become superfluous does qualify as a possibility and not just a form of words.

The female stick insect can, somehow, activate its own eggs without any need for a male at all. The offspring are all female. If we discovered how the stick insect does this then women would not need a male at all. They could activate their own eggs and produce female children. So it is just a possibility.

So there has to be some evidence for something to qualify as a possibility and not just a form of words.

The second step up the ratings ladder is for something to be plausible. This is more than 'just a possibility'. There is enough evidence to make a possibility worth considering.

At this stage, to think about the possibility or to talk about the possibility is not unreasonable.

As the evidence increases something becomes 'probable'.

Probable has two meanings.

The first meaning is that there is sufficient evidence to believe that something is a strong enough possibility to become likely or probable. The reference is to the supporting evidence.

The second meaning of probable is a 'competitive' one. This means that this possibility is more probable than the other possibilities. The reference is now to the competing options.

The obvious danger is that as soon as we begin to think that one possibility is more probable than the others, we ignore the others and only look for evidence to support our choice.

From a thinking point of view, the important point is to seek evidence for other possibilities – even when you consider one of them to be more probable.

In romance terms, keep romancing all the other girls even when you think you have chosen your favourite. This might make you a playboy. That is exactly how your thinking should work!

The final rating is 'proved'. This is the stage we want to get to before action or judgement. The possibility has moved from being a possibility to something that has been proved.

There is no dispute about the end point of thinking needing to be proved (if possible). It is the way to get to that end point that matters. On the way we need to generate and consider all sorts of possibilities – not just to stay with the probabilities all along. You may have to go south at some point in order to go north in the end.

The ratings might be:

Possible (p)
Plausible (pp)
Probable (ppp)
Proved (pppp)

There is no harm at all in using these (pp, etc.) ratings. They can be very helpful.

We must, however, consciously avoid the temptation to throw out the low (p) ratings. In fact, we ought to give them rather more attention.

It is the lower ratings (p) that are likely to change our thinking. The higher rating ones are likely to confirm our existing thinking.

POSSIBILITIES AND FREEDOM

I once wrote a book with the title *Are you Americans Really Free?* (Published 2007 by New Millennium Publishers.)

Everyone knows that America is the land of the free. The generosity of the American spirit in helping others to be free is well known. The Statue of Liberty symbolizes this freedom.

Freedom is the absence of tyranny, control and oppression. There is no doubt that America qualifies on this basis.

But can you have freedom without possibilities?

Women travel with rather large suitcases — to the great annoyance of their male companions. Men do not understand the need for so much luggage.

If, however, there is one single evening reception on the trip then the woman has to lay out five outfits in order to be free to choose one of them. If she had only packed one outfit that is not freedom to choose.

If there is but one road between two towns you take that road. If there are many roads and you know about them all, then you are free to choose one of them.

If there are many roads but you only know one of them, are you free?

America only knows about one set of values and one way of life — because these are the best. Are you free to choose these if you know of no others? You can argue that you do not need to know about inferior ways of life. Trust me: this is the best one.

If you have no choice of career but have to follow in the footsteps of your father then you have no freedom — even if this is actually the best choice.

When you set out to buy a house do you open up all the possibilities: large or small, country or town, modern or traditional, etc.? Or, do you specify your choice very exactly and then look for what you know you want?

Women looking for husbands or men looking for wives have the same difficulty. Should you know exactly what you are looking for – or should you entertain different possibilities?

Once again there is the difficulty between the 'thinking stage' and the 'action stage' that has been repeated throughout the book.

Does freedom need possibilities?

CONCLUSION

This book has been about the huge importance of 'possibilities'.

Without possibilities we are not likely to make progress.

We need possibilities of explanation and understanding, as in the hypotheses of science and the understanding of social data.

We need possibilities in the design of the way forward in strategies, in legislation and in behaviour.

At the end we want as much certainty as possible for our judgements and actions.

But on the way to that 'end' we need to be able to generate multiple possibilities and to examine them fully and honestly.

The nature of our thinking at the end does not need to be the same as the nature of the thinking that gets us to the end.

Without possibilities we stagnate in yesterday's certainties.